FIRST
PEOPLES
of NORTH
AMERICA

THE PEOPLE AND CULTURE OF THE

DELAWARE

RAYMOND BIAL

Cavendish
Square

New York

Published in 2016 by Cavendish Square Publishing, LLC
243 5th Avenue, Suite 136, New York, NY 10016

Library of Congress Cataloging-in-Publication Data

Bial, Raymond.
[Delaware.]
The people and culture of the Delaware / Raymond Bial.
pages cm. — (First peoples of North America)
Includes bibliographical references and index.
ISBN 978-1-5026-1004-1 (hardcover) ISBN 978-1-5026-1005-8 (ebook)
1. Delaware Indians—History—Juvenile literature.
2. Delaware Indians—Social life and customs—Juvenile literature. I. Title.
E99.D2B53 2016
974.004'97345—dc23

2015023313

Editorial Director: David McNamara
Editor: Kristen Susienka
Copy Editor: Nathan Heidelberger
Art Director: Jeffrey Talbot
Designer: Amy Greenan
Senior Production Manager: Jennifer Ryder-Talbot
Production Editor: Renni Johnson
Photo Research: J8 Media

The photographs in this book are used by permission and through the courtesy of: Public Domain/National Anthropological Archives, Smithsonian Institution, Washington/Lenape01.jpg/Wikimedia Commons, cover, 31; AP Photo/Shawano Leader, Cory Dellenbach, back cover; Shawano Leader, Cory Dellenbach/AP Photo, 6; MPI/Getty Images, 8; MyLoupe/UIG via Getty Images, 12; North Wind Picture Archives, 14, 16, 35, 68, 72; Raymond Bial, 15, 24-25, 33, 51, 52, 54, 58, 60, 81, 82-83, 84, 109; http://en.wikipedia.org/wiki/File:Delaware01.png/Wikimedia Commons, 18; Kean Collection/Getty Images, 20; Marilyn Angel Wynn/Native Stock Pictures, 23, 37, 66, 90, 94; MyLoupe/UIG Via Getty Images, 26; Hollar, Wenceslaus/Virginia Historical Society, Richmond, Virginia, USA/Bridgeman Images, 27; MEPL/Alamy, 28; Embleton, Ron/Private Collection/Look and Learn/Bridgeman Images, 38-39; Cjmckendry/iStockphoto.com, 41; Jascha Asadov/Shutterstock.com, 45; Public Domain/Susie Elkhair-Deleware Tribe of Indians-(Lenape).jpg/Wikimedia Commons, 47; Kean Collection/Getty Images, 56; Maks Narodenko/Shutterstock.com, 62; Public Domain/Historical Society of Pennsylvania/Moravian mission.jpg/Wikimedia Commons, 74; Popperfoto/Getty Images, 77; National Geographic Image Collection/Alamy, 87; Jeff Vele/Mohican News, 89; Jake Rajs/Getty Images, 93; Kean Collection/Getty Images, 97; James Rementer/Noradean.jpg/Wikimedia Commons, 98; Public Domain/CharlesJourneycake1854.jpg/Wikimedia Commons, 101; MPI/Getty Images, 102; Smallbones/Gettysburg mon NY Tammany Reg.JPG/Wikimedia Commons, 106.

Printed in the United States of America

ACKNOWLEDGMENTS

The People and Culture of the Delaware would not have been possible without the help of a number of individuals and organizations. I would especially like to thank the Delaware Tribe of Indians and the many hospitable people in Oklahoma who allowed me to make photographs at their powwow near Bartlesville and made my visit so enjoyable.

I would also like to thank Cavendish Square Publishing for their help and support. As always, I offer my deepest appreciation to my wife, Linda, and my children, Anna, Sarah, and Luke, for their support in the research, writing, and photography for this book.

CONTENTS

A man dressed in traditional clothes dances at the grand entry of the Stockbridge Munsee Tribe's Veteran Powwow in August 2006.

AUTHOR'S NOTE

At the dawn of the twentieth century, Native Americans were thought to be a vanishing race. However, despite four hundred years of warfare, deprivation, and disease, Native Americans have persevered. Countless thousands have lost their lives, but over the course of this century and the last, the populations of Native tribes have grown tremendously. Even as America's First Peoples struggle to adapt to modern Western life, they have also kept the flame of their traditions alive—the languages, religions, stories, and the everyday ways of life. An exhilarating renaissance in Native American culture is now sweeping the continent from coast to coast.

The First Peoples of North America books depict the social and cultural life of the major nations, from the early history of Native peoples in North America to their present-day struggles for survival and dignity. Historical and contemporary photographs of traditional subjects, as well as period illustrations, are blended throughout each book so that readers may gain a sense of family life in a tipi, a hogan, or a longhouse.

No single book can comprehensively portray the intricate and varied lifeways of an entire tribe, or nation. I only hope that young people will come away with a deeper appreciation for the rich tapestry of Native American culture—both then and now—and a keen desire to learn more about these first Americans.

This illustration shows Delaware tribe members resting during the American Civil War.

CHAPTER ONE

[Many] believed that the Delaware were the original tribe of the Algonquian-speaking peoples.

A CULTURE BEGINS

For centuries, North America has been home to many different groups of people called Native Americans. Ancestors of these men, women, and children originated in Asia and crossed the Bering Strait thousands of years ago. They eventually branched out and established communities in other parts of the vast continent, forming individual groups called nations, bands, or tribes. Today these groups still exist, although they have had to endure much struggle and hardship to remain. One such group is now called the Delaware.

Becoming the Delaware

Delaware (DEL-a-ware) was the name given in the early years of the seventeenth century to several bands of Native people, related by language and culture, who lived in the valley of the Delaware River and nearby. Few of these bands were united politically, but they all shared many traditions, including storytelling, which helped to keep their history and customs alive. One origin story recounts how the Creator made the Earth on the back of a giant turtle. Other stories describe how the Delaware provided for themselves. The following story emphasizes the importance of corn in the lives of these people:

> Mother Corn was thought to be a living, womanlike spirit. However, in the days of old, several boys mocked this belief. "Corn cannot possibly leave the Earth," they claimed, but then Mother Corn vanished, and the people faced the danger of a great **famine**.
>
> A person blessed with a token from the Great Spirit explained, "Unless we find someone to coax Mother Corn to return to Earth, the people will starve to death."
>
> The people learned that the boys had joked about the spirit of corn, but no one could figure out how to bring her back. This was a great mystery, and the people endured a famine for a year.

Then two boys of scant means learned of the trouble. They came to a gathering of the people and offered to help them. These boys had spiritual powers but did not say how they would approach Mother Corn.

As the people were sitting in a ring at night, the boys departed. They went to a place above the Earth, where they made a burnt offering out of a mussel shell and asked Mother Corn to come back to Earth. Moved by their sacrifice, Mother Corn appeared to the boys and said that she would honor their request. The boys returned to the people with this good news. They brought a handful of corn with them and pledged that Mother Corn would never leave again.

Thereafter, corn was raised in abundance. Because of the spiritual power of the two boys, Mother Corn has never broken her promise and remains with the people to this day. Since Mother Corn took the form of a woman, it is the women who tend the fields, harvest and husk the ears, and store the corn for the people.

For countless generations the Delaware lived in small groups and bands in the Delaware Valley and parts of Pennsylvania, New Jersey, and New York. They referred to themselves as the **Lenape** (lun-NAH-pay), which means "ordinary, real, or original people." The term Delaware derived from the title of Sir Thomas West, Lord de la Warr, the first governor of the English colony at Jamestown, Virginia. When one of his followers,

The Delaware River Valley is full of beautiful scenery.

Captain Samuel Argall, was exploring the Atlantic coast north of Jamestown in 1610, he sailed into a magnificent bay, which he named de la Warr Bay in honor of the governor. Governor West apparently was not impressed with the honor and returned to England without ever visiting the bay. However, English colonists later came to use Delaware as a name for the bay, the river flowing into it, and the Lenape people who lived there. The name Delaware later came to refer to nearly all Lenape people.

The Lenape did not generally object to being called the Delaware, but they had their own story about the origin of the name. According to this story, when the English first arrived in North America, they asked a Lenape the name of the tribe to which he belonged, and he repeatedly answered, "Lenape." The Englishman mispronounced the word, saying, "Lenuhpee" or "Renahpay." Finally he managed to mutter Lenape correctly, and the Lenape cried, "Nal në ndëluwèn! Nal në ndëluwèn!" which means, "That's what I said! That's what I said!" However, the Englishman heard only dëluwèn and he responded, "So you are a Delaware. Now I know what to call you." The name has persisted for nearly four hundred years. The Delaware accept the name when speaking with non–Native Americans, who often cannot pronounce Lenape properly. However, when speaking to each other, they proudly refer to themselves as Lenape.

Before the arrival of Europeans, Delaware bands lived peacefully in scattered villages. The men hunted game, while the women tended their fields of corn, beans, and squash. People often came together for religious celebrations and occasionally to wage war.

For many **Algonquian**-speaking peoples, the Delaware were honored as the "grandfathers." They believed that the Delaware were the original tribe of all the Algonquian-speaking peoples. They were respected as peacemakers, who wisely settled disputes between rival tribes. However, when they had to fight, they were well known for their courage and skill as warriors.

Encountering Europeans

In the early 1600s, the Delaware were among the first Native Americans to encounter Europeans along the Atlantic coast. Florentine explorer Giovanni da Verrazano, who sailed along the Atlantic coast in 1524, was the first known European to venture into their territory. However, the Delaware were not seriously

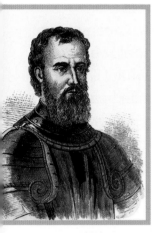

Giovanni da Verrazano

affected by Europeans until Henry Hudson sailed into New York Harbor in 1609. It is estimated there were about forty bands with a total population of eight thousand to twelve thousand Delaware people at the time. Soon, Dutch and Swedish immigrants were peacefully settling in what is now southern New Jersey and the state of Delaware. The Delaware traded beaver pelts with the newcomers for metal goods—mainly pots, kettles, and tools—along with guns, cloth, and glass beads. The Europeans offered many useful goods, but they also introduced alcohol, which greatly harmed the Delaware and other Native peoples.

In their first dealings with Europeans, the Delaware chose the "path of peace." Having no concept that their land could be owned, they readily signed treaties, which they regarded generally as leases, not sales contracts. They believed that the land belonged to the Creator and that people were simply allowed to harvest its bounty of food and materials to use for clothing and shelter. When the weary Europeans straggled off their ships after their long voyage and needed a place to live, the Delaware generously shared the land with them. When the colonists offered gifts, the Delaware believed that they were simply being repaid for their

The Delaware grew many crops, including corn.

hospitality. However, the Europeans regarded these gifts as payment for the land.

The Delaware and Swedes tended to peacefully share with each other their knowledge and skills in hunting, farming, and handicrafts. The Swedes taught the Native Americans how to construct sturdy log cabins and weave splint baskets from strips of hardwood. In return, the Delaware showed the settlers how to grow an abundance of corn and how to fill their nets with fish in nearby streams and rivers. However, the Delaware became overly dependent on Dutch trade items, such as durable brass kettles and duffel cloth, which was lighter than **buckskin**. Many of the Delaware also became addicted to liquor.

Their yearning for trade goods prompted the Delaware to wantonly hunt and trap animals only for their pelts. This new practice, the loss of their ancestral lands, and epidemics of diseases against which Native Americans had little resistance soon devastated their population and changed their lives forever.

Prior to Europeans arriving, the Delaware used animals such as deer to make clothes, weapons, and tools.

Where the Delaware Lived

At one time, the vast territory of the Delaware included all of what is now New Jersey, eastern Pennsylvania, southeastern New York State, northern Delaware, and a small portion of southeastern Connecticut. They had no general name for this territory, but in recent years it has sometimes been called **Lenapehoking**, which means "Land of the Lenape."

In the northern half of the territory—north of a line that runs east to west about halfway between Philadelphia and New York City—the people spoke a Delaware language called **Munsee**. The Munsee bands included the Esopus, who made their home west of the Hudson River between the Catskill Mountains and the highlands at what is now West Point. These Esopus people were composed of a number of small bands, notably the Waoranecks and Waranawankongs.

Other Munsee groups were the Minisink, who lived on the Delaware River; also the Haverstraw and the Tappan, just west of the Hudson and south of the Esopus Creek. East of the Hudson were the Wappinger, and south of the Wappinger, several bands in what is now Westchester County, including the Kichtawank, the Sinsink, and the Wiechquaeskeck. Another band, the Rechgawawanks, lived in the Bronx and Manhattan. To the west—on western Long Island—were the Nayack, the Marechikawieck, the Canarsee, and the Rockaway.

Still other Munsee bands lived in northern New Jersey— the Hackensack, the Navesink, and the Raritan. The Raritan made their home on the lower Raritan River, although in the 1640s they were driven farther inland by a hostile band from the Delaware River to the west and by the Dutch.

South of the Munsee were the Delaware who spoke **Unami**, a language that at one time had at least three major dialects—Southern Unami, Northern Unami, and Unalachtigo. In New Jersey the Unami bands included the Sewapois along the Cohansey River; the Little Siconese along the Salem River; the Naraticonck along Raccoon Creek; the Armewamex on Big and Little Timber Creeks; the Remkokes on Rancocas Creek; the Atsayonck along Crosswicks Creek; and the Sankhikan, who lived near the falls at Trenton, New Jersey.

On the west bank of the Delaware River in what is now the state of Delaware, the only known group was the Big Siconese. Between the Big Siconese and the present-day city of Philadelphia were two other bands, the Minguannan on White Clay Creek and the

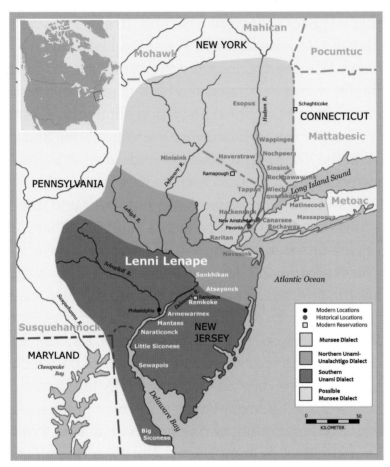

This map shows the different languages spoken by Delaware tribes.

Quineomessinque on the big bend of Brandywine Creek. Most likely, attacks by the Susquehannock—an Iroquoian tribe from the Susquehanna River to the west—had devastated their villages and seriously reduced the Delaware population. Later in the 1600s, in this part of Pennsylvania, the village of Playwicky was established on Upper Neshaminy Creek, along with the settlements of the Okehocking band on Ridley and Crum Creeks.

Of particular interest are the Unami groups who lived along the Delaware River between Tohickon Creek—

about 30 miles (48 kilometers) north of Philadelphia—
and present-day Burlington—about 15 miles (24 km)
downstream from Trenton, New Jersey. These people,
who were closely allied politically, spoke Southern
Unami—the Unami dialect that has survived among the
Delaware people now living in Oklahoma after a long
history of forced relocation.

The sprawling homeland of these many bands varied
widely in climate and geography. The territory included
the windswept coastal plains and flat, marshy lowlands
of what are now eastern Delaware and New Jersey. It
also embraced the rolling, forested hills of southeastern
Pennsylvania and the rocky terrain of northern New
Jersey and southeastern New York. The region was
marked by the Delaware and Hudson rivers, whose
many tributaries reached far inland and branched into
numerous streams. These creeks originated in springs
often hundreds of miles from where the mouth of the
river flowed into the Atlantic Ocean.

While the bands of Delaware were connected
through language and culture, they developed their own
habits and communities based on the environments in
which they lived. The Delaware of the north wore warm
clothing and built dwellings that could withstand cold
temperatures. Bands farther south, on the other hand,
wore less clothing and crafted cooler buildings to keep
out warmer weather. Yet for hundreds of years the bands
not only survived but prospered in a land that abounded
in game, fish, and edible plants. Their determination and
persistence has ensured their survival for all this time.
Even today, their nation continues to exist.

The early Delaware people formed thriving civilizations.

*Our ancestors are part
of the grass and trees.*

—Ron Welburn,
Lenape/Cherokee/
African American
and professor

BUILDING A CIVILIZATION

Early Delaware groups built communities throughout the eastern United States. These were structured places where people could raise a family, hunt for food, and spend long winter months. By the time Europeans arrived, the Delaware civilization was a thriving network sharing heritage, language, and family.

Delaware Communities

In the seventeenth century, the Delaware lived in bands centered around settled villages, ranging in size from as few as fourteen to as many as two or three hundred people. However, most people lived in small bands of twenty-five or thirty people.

Their dwellings were scattered in the woods or strung out along a riverbank, with no semblance of a plan for streets or a public square. Moreover, until the arrival of Europeans, the houses were usually not surrounded by a **palisade** or fortified in any manner. Every ten or twelve years, when they had exhausted the soil in their fields and most of the game had been hunted, the band moved the entire village.

People were related by family and **clan**, and they regarded themselves as members of their community. Within the village they felt a sense of responsibility toward others and generally treated each other kindly. Village property, including farm fields, belonged to the clan leaders, as did the rights to seasonal ceremonies held in that town. Food and shelter were often shared, and individuals rarely hoarded valuable property.

The Delaware had strong bonds between parents and children, and among all related members of the clans. Like their neighbors the Mahican, Mohawk, and Oneida, they had three clans. Among the Delaware, these were called Turtle (Pukuangu), Turkey (Pële), and Wolf (Tùkwsit). Both family kinship and clan membership were traced through the mother. Children were born into their mother's clan. They belonged to their mother, and were raised and educated by her brothers. The father looked after his sisters' children, not his own, although family ties were strong and loving.

A clan group in the village usually included an elder woman known as a clan matron, her sisters and brothers, her sons and daughters, and her daughters' children. Although a son remained a member of his mother's clan, he had to marry a woman from another

Three Nanticoke children attend a powwow.

clan. When a man married, he moved into the home of his wife's parents, and their children belonged to the mother's clan.

Buildings and Shelter

Delaware houses varied in size and shape depending on the season and location, but there were generally three styles: round with a domed roof, oblong with an arched roof, and oblong with a ridge-pole and a pitched roof. All were made of bark and branches, readily available in the forests around them. In the northern range they preferred rectangular, bark-covered longhouses with rounded ends and a door on the side. Several related families generally lived in each of these dwellings. In the southern part of their territory the Delaware tended to live in dome-shaped, mat-covered houses, or wigwams, large enough for a single family.

Longhouses were about 20 feet (6 meters) wide and could be over 100 feet (30.5 m) long. A longhouse with an average length of 60 feet (18.3 m) could shelter seven or eight families. Longhouses were clustered in winter settlements, often on hilltops and—after the arrival of Europeans—within a palisade wall of pointed, vertical logs. If not protected by a stockade, longhouses tended to be scattered throughout a wide territory.

To construct these long, oval-shaped buildings, the Delaware first made an arched frame by setting flexible green hickory saplings into the ground in pairs opposite each other. The saplings were bent toward each other and lashed together to form the arch. Horizontal poles were then tied across this framework. This structure was covered with large sheets of bark, as long as 6 feet

The People and Culture of the Delaware

The Delaware built shelters out of trees and animal hides.

(1.8 m). They left an opening, about 1 foot (0.3 m) wide, along the crown of the longhouse, which served as a smoke hole, and a small opening for a doorway at each end. A row of fires, one for each family, ran down the middle of the earth floor on the inside. Down the length of the dwelling, people hung kettles on horizontal poles suspended from forked posts over these fires. Families also partitioned off their living space within the longhouse.

Especially during the summer, when people often moved, the Delaware made small houses that were situated near their cornfields, fishing camps, and seasonal hunting grounds. The wooden frames of these dome-shaped houses were sheathed with mats woven from reeds, with a smoke hole at the top and a small doorway in the side. People also furnished these houses with woven mats, which covered the floor and hung from the walls. Mats on the walls were painted with decorations. The homes of chiefs featured designs of faces and other images that suggested the dwellings were also used for religious ceremonies.

This wigwam is an example of a Delaware house.

The Delaware also constructed **sweat lodges**, large enough for three or four men, near a stream or river. Small branches covered these structures, which were then sealed with clay.

In their villages women tended the cooking fires, tanned animal skins, and wove baskets, as well as **hoed** the cornfields. The men were often away catching game, birds, and fish for their families, including elderly parents. They also undertook some of the heavy work around the village, such as building the frame for a house, making dugout canoes, fashioning mortars and pestles for grinding corn, and crafting bows and arrows.

The People and Culture of the Delaware

Tribal Governing

The Delaware way of life changed dramatically from the seventeenth to twenty-first centuries, which makes it hard to determine the social and political relationships that existed originally. It is known that bands at times acted independently, yet they often cooperated in hunting, warfare, and diplomacy with the Iroquois and Europeans. Individual bands also agreed upon territorial rights for hunting, fishing, and oystering. Leaders arranged for marriages between members of different bands as well. To strengthen their bonds of friendship, they frequently traveled to other villages to visit with each other.

Each band had two leaders—a clan chief and a war chief. The war chief achieved his position through courage and skill in battle. A proven war chief could gather young warriors and go on a raid without the approval of the clan chief. The clan chief mediated conflicts and arranged ceremonies and group activities. He usually directed large hunts in which groups surrounded and drove game with the aid of fire. He also oversaw legal duties, such as pursuing murderers and ensuring

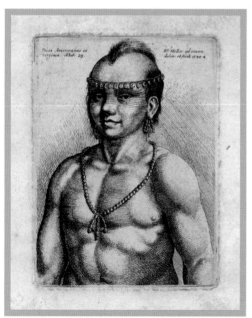

This illustration from 1645 shows a man named Jacques, who was from the Munsee Delaware Tribe.

Each Delaware
community had a
chief, such as this one.

payment of wampum, or shell money. Traditionally,
a clan chief did not wield much authority beyond
persuasion. He could not control warriors and served
primarily as a spokesman in dealings with Europeans.
However, by the last decades of the seventeenth
century, chiefs achieved greater power over united
bands as they dealt with Europeans encroaching on
their territory. Some leaders, such as Oratimin of the
Hackensack and Tappan, became prominent chiefs of
united bands that lived in the same territory.

Major decisions were made by a general council,
which William Penn described as "all the Old and Wise

men of [the] Nation, which perhaps is two hundred people." This council also included all the young men, but occasionally chiefs might seek advice from a group that included women and children, too. Certain families might have rights to hunting territory, but the entire group apparently had to decide whether or not to give up their land.

A chief could designate a successor from within the clan. However, his choice was not binding after he resigned or died. Succession generally followed the mother's side of the family, but there were cases in which a new chief was chosen from the father's line. Chiefs were chosen for their good conduct, public speaking skills, honesty, and wisdom in decision making. They also had to be knowledgeable about their religion, since they led rituals and ceremonies.

Some of the easternmost Delaware bands had a priest, like the religious leaders, called powwows, of eastern Long Island and New England. However, in most Delaware bands the chief also acted as the religious leader.

The Delaware Nation created a more stationary society than other Native groups within North America. They moved only when they had to and spent much of their time in communities brought together by kinship. They treated the land with respect and helped one another. When Europeans arrived, the Delaware lent them their help, too. However, that changed as more and more settlers came to dwell in their territory, taking the land the Delaware had worked so hard to care for.

After Europeans arrived, many Native Americans started to wear Western clothes.

CHAPTER THREE

The Delaware made, or traded for, all the objects they needed.

LIFE IN THE DELAWARE NATION

The Delaware Nation lived in communities, and each community had certain rituals they celebrated, foods they made, and crafts they created. Many of these activities were similar throughout each Delaware tribe and shaped the way men, women, and children lived their lives from day to day.

The Life Cycle

In their daily lives, the Delaware followed the cycle of the seasons—counting the months by the changing moon—which determined the chores to be undertaken and the rituals to be held at those times. Everyone worked, but women and men had clearly defined tasks. Women planted crops, gathered wild foods, and made baskets, while the men hunted, fished, and crafted tools. Women gave birth, men became fathers, and old people told stories drawn from deep within their memories. Children simply followed the example of their parents and grandparents as they grew up, married, and raised families of their own.

Being Born

When a woman was about to give birth, she retired to a small hut away from the other dwellings in the village. She washed the baby with cold water. The newborn was then wrapped onto a **cradleboard**, where it remained for about one year. A woman carried the cradleboard on her back with a tumpline, or strap, around her forehead. While the mother worked, she propped the cradleboard beside the dwelling or against a tree so her infant could watch her. Once her baby outgrew the cradleboard, the mother carried the child in an animal skin drawn around her shoulders. Babies were nursed for one to two years, after which they were fed a corn soup.

Children

From an early age, children were given daily tasks. Girls helped around the dwelling and in the fields. Boys learned to catch fish and hunt birds and small game

This mask shows the face of a guardian spirit.

with bows and arrows. These activities helped children to acquire the skills they would need to thrive as adults.

At puberty, a boy went on a **vision quest** to find the spirit that would serve as his guide through life. Once a young man recognized his guardian spirit, he made an amulet, or sacred object, that represented the spirit. He never revealed his vision until he reached manhood. In the meantime, he followed the ways of his elders and sought a humble and prayerful manner. Among the Delaware, humility was an esteemed virtue. A girl similarly called upon helpful spirits in times of ill health or other trouble.

When a girl had her first menstruation, she retired to a special hut until she had her second period. During this time she kept a blanket over her head and avoided touching her hair. Also not allowed to touch food or utensils, she ate with a stick and drank water with her cupped hands. Thereafter, she followed similar practices whenever she had her period.

After her first seclusion, a young woman wore a special headdress and wampum that indicated that she was now an adult. When they had learned all the skills necessary to support a family, both young women and young men were considered ready to be married.

Marrying

If a young man wished to marry a certain young woman, he approached her directly or spoke to her friends or parents. If his proposal of marriage was accepted, he then offered strings of wampum as a gift. The couple was engaged for one year, during which the woman continued to wear her headdress and wampum. After this betrothal period there was a great feast, but no other ceremony, after which the couple was considered to be married.

The couple lived with the bride's mother before moving into a home of their own, where the wife managed the household affairs. Most couples had a marriage bundle, a pouch or handkerchief that held small figures of a man and woman along with herbs and medicines. It was believed that the bundle had spiritual power to keep the husband and wife together. However, if a couple did not get along, they could easily divorce and marry another person if they wished.

Dying

A few days after a person died, the body was washed and dressed in fine clothes. The hair was combed, and the face was painted red. The body was then placed in a shallow grave in a sitting position. Some graves were isolated, while others were located in a cemetery near the village. Graves were lined with bark, tree limbs, or animal skins. Tools and utensils were put inside, along with the food and wampum that the deceased would need in the afterlife. Branches were then placed around the body, and the grave was covered with soil, heaped with stones, and enclosed with a fence.

At some time during the funeral, people held a feast in honor of the deceased. Erected over the grave was a post with pictures that depicted the abilities and heroic deeds of the deceased. Mourners blackened their faces as a sign of respect. Widows might crawl about the grave and burn their hair as an expression of their deep grief. Mourners did not speak the name of the dead person, so as not to hurt the feelings of the family of the deceased. Spouses mourned for a full year. A widower might then offer payment to his wife's relatives, to be free to marry again. Thereafter, mourners visited the burial site every year to tend the grave, removing grass and leaves.

Warring

Before the arrival of Dutch and English colonists, the
Delaware often carried on long wars with the Iroquois-
speaking peoples who lived in what is now northern
New York. At the time, the Delaware were generally too
powerful for the five Iroquois nations. However, when
European traders provided firearms to the Mohawk
(one of the Iroquois nations) but not to the Delaware,
the situation changed dramatically, and the Delaware

The People and Culture of the Delaware

The Iroquois tribes fought with the Delaware and eventually pushed them out of their homeland.

faced dangerous confrontations with their enemies. The Delaware also sometimes fought with other villages in disputes over hunting and fishing territories. Captives were either tortured and killed or adopted into the tribe.

In preparation for battle, warriors donned special clothing, painted their faces, and chanted war songs. Warriors then danced before they went on a raid or into a war. Weapons included long bows strung with braided sinew, which stood as tall as a man, and arrows made of wooden shafts tipped with stone points. Men made points, or arrowheads, by chipping small pieces of flint or other stones that flaked easily into triangular shapes. Instead of flint, men occasionally used sharp bones, horns, or the teeth of animals or fish as arrowheads. They stuck a finished arrowhead onto the end of a feathered shaft with fish glue or pine resin and then tied it securely with sinew. Men also crafted heavy wooden clubs, which they wielded during close fighting. For protection they wore wooden helmets

A Lenni Lenape war club with sharp points made from obsidian

and held large, rectangular shields made of wood or moose hide.

Bands occasionally came together for a major raid or war, although these conflicts were always limited in nature. There was enough land and food for everyone, and people could trade for any other objects they needed. However, after the arrival of Europeans, competition for land and trade goods quickly intensified. Tribes began to compete for control of the fur trade. With a small, scattered population and no centrally organized political government, the Delaware were not prepared to unite as one nation to resist either the European colonists or the strengthened nations of the Iroquois **Confederacy**, who sought to push them from their ancestral lands.

Food

The Delaware hunted throughout the year but mostly in the late fall. Every year after the leaves had fallen they burned the undergrowth in the forest. They used these fires to drive or trap game during large, communal hunts known as surrounds. In the open woods it was easier to track game. The fires also kept abandoned fields near the village from growing over again.

During the winter they dispersed and lived in small camps scattered throughout the woods, although in times of war they might take refuge in hilltop villages. In April they burned any areas that had been missed in the previous fall and, if necessary, cleared new fields near their villages. The women then planted corn and other crops, after which people went to trade with other tribes or the European settlers. Some families journeyed to the nesting places of passenger pigeons and collected young birds, called squabs. During the spring and summer they also caught fish and shellfish in the ocean. Often the women planted gardens at the places where they regularly fished and where the men went hunting.

Using bows and arrows—and guns when they later became available—the men hunted many kinds of game, including deer, elk, black bears, raccoons, beavers, fishers, otters, and rabbits, for meat, skins, and sinew. Moose were occasionally hunted, too. Beavers and other small game were often trapped. However, the deer was the most important game animal. Bands often organized hunting parties of one hundred to two hundred people and surrounded the deer with fire or

The Delaware were connected to the land and animals, such as deer.

drove the animals into a natural impasse, such as a river. Deer hides were used for making clothing, and sinew was used for binding arrowheads, for thread, and for other purposes. Bear fat was melted down, purified in a sacred ritual, and stored in skin bags.

Hunters also killed birds—mostly turkeys, ducks, geese, and passenger pigeons—for their meat and feathers. Sometimes they ate eggs gathered from nests. Birds such as geese and ducks were shot with bows and arrows as they touched down in marshes. These migratory birds were also caught in traps and nets. The turkey was the most important game bird of the forests and fields. The Delaware especially liked the flavor of the meat, and women fashioned elaborate, colorful robes and mantles with turkey feathers. They tied the feathers onto a handmade net backing, which was then fastened to a skin cloak worn over the shoulders. The passenger pigeon was also a vitally important game bird. As thousands of these birds flew over the land in enormous flocks the men caught the birds in nets. They also raided the nests for eggs and squabs. Later, non-Native hunters killed so many passenger pigeons that by the beginning of the twentieth century they became extinct.

Fishing provided an abundance of food for the Delaware. Some lakes and rivers could be fished all year long. However, many fish—such as eels, herring, shad, salmon, and sturgeons—migrated to the ocean during the cold winter months and returned up the rivers to spawn, or lay their eggs, during the spring. Every year, thousands of shad swam more than 300 miles (483 km) from the Atlantic Ocean into the Delaware, Raritan, Passaic, and Hudson Rivers to lay their eggs. To catch fish, the Delaware relied on weirs, fence-like traps set up from one bank to the other, or dragged long, weighted nets through the water. They also used small nets, hooks and lines, and bows and arrows to catch fish. Most fish were fairly easy to catch, but sturgeons could be over 6 feet (1.8 m) long and weigh more than 200 pounds (91 kilograms). Men sometimes used harpoons tipped with the branches of deer antlers to spear these large, ancient-looking fish, which were then wrestled onto land.

Fresh fish were slowly roasted over a fire. Women also wrapped fish in soft clay and baked them in hot ashes. The clay acted like an oven to evenly cook the flesh. When the clay had hardened, it was broken away, and the fish was ready to eat. Even the skin and scales tended to come off with the baked clay. Fish eggs, or roe, were a special treat.

Delaware bands that lived near the coast gathered clams, oysters, and scallops along the shore and in the bays. In fact, these people harvested and ate huge amounts of the succulent shellfish. Those who lived farther inland along lakes, rivers, and streams gathered and ate freshwater mussels. They also caught and ate crayfish, a small freshwater version of the lobster.

The forests, meadows, and waters so abounded in game that the Delaware could readily provide for themselves and their families through all the seasons. People usually caught more game and fish than they could eat at a time, so they dried the surplus in the sun or smoked it over a wood fire. It could then be stored and eaten later in the year. Meat and fish that had been smoked or dried in the sun lasted for many months, often longer. Strips of this meat could be slowly chewed, or pieces could be added to soups or stews.

Through the spring, summer, and fall, women and children went into the forests to gather wild plants: leaves, roots, berries, fruits, and nuts, along with mushrooms. Many of these foods, especially sweet berries, were eaten as soon as they ripened. The rest could be dried and stored for the wintertime.

In the spring women and children picked wild strawberries, blueberries, and blackberries. In the summer they dug the roots of cattail plants and water lilies and collected persimmons, cranberries, and wild plums. Nuts, such as walnuts, butternuts, hickory nuts, and chestnuts, were gathered in October and November. Women also filled baskets with acorns from oak trees. To remove the bitter taste, they crushed the nuts in a wooden mortar then rinsed the coarse meal in hot water. The leached acorn meal was then cooked in porridge or used as flour to make bread. Cooking oil was also obtained from nuts, which were crushed and boiled. As the nut meal boiled, the oil was released and floated to the top of the water, where it was skimmed off with spoons or ladles made from turtle shells or clamshells. Nut oil was stored in gourd bottles or clay pots until needed.

In the fields near their homes, women carefully planted corn, beans, squash, sunflowers, and a few herbs. Men often grew a little tobacco, which was used in rituals. Corn was the most important crop, with a few seeds planted in each of the hills dotting the fields. Women then planted several different kinds of beans, which grew up the cornstalks. They also grew squash, which wound around the clumps of corn and beans.

Vegetables were harvested and eaten fresh as soon as they were ripe. However, much of the harvest had to be stored away for the lean months of winter. Ears of corn could be stored in woven baskets or simply tied in bundles and hung from the house rafters to dry in the heat and smoke of cooking fires. Dried corn kernels and shelled beans could also be stored in skin bags or baskets. Pumpkins and squash were cut into rings, which were placed on a stick and dried in the sun or over the smoke of a fire.

The Delaware also dug caches, or storage pits, in the ground near their homes and lined them with hemp mats. Dried meat, fish, corn, nuts, and other foods were placed in these pits, and helped people survive the long, cold winter. These foods would not spoil as long as they remained dry. When a woman wanted to use dried food, she simply cooked it in water. The dried food absorbed some of the water, swelled up, and softened enough to become an ingredient in a dish.

Cooking

The Delaware generously shared their food with others, so no one ever went hungry as long as there was some food in the village. There were no fixed times for meals, but generally people ate in the morning and the evening. Every day, people ate cornmeal mush, often flavored with a little dried and pounded meat or fish. They boiled or roasted fresh meat or fish on sticks set in the ground near the fire. To make bread, women often wrapped cornmeal in husks, which they then baked in hot ashes. They enjoyed several delicacies, including beaver tails, striped bass heads, fat meat with chestnuts, and finely ground parched corn. They often sweetened foods with berries.

Today, the Delaware enjoy a wide variety of popular foods, including pizza, hamburgers, fried chicken, and beefsteak. However, on special occasions they serve traditional foods such as grape dumplings.

Clothes and Accessories

Before Europeans established colonies along the Atlantic coast, Delaware men wore only a buckskin **breechcloth** and **moccasins** in warm weather. They sometimes put on buckskin leggings during colder weather or if they were venturing into heavy brush. During warm weather, women wore only moccasins

RECIPE

SHËWAHSAPAN (GRAPE DUMPLINGS)

INGREDIENTS

6 cups (1420 milliliters) grape juice

About 1 cup (237 mL) sugar, to taste

1 tablespoon (15 mL) butter

About 3 cups (710 mL) flour

Slowly heat grape juice and sugar in a large saucepan, reserving 1 to 1.5 cups (237 to 355 mL) grape juice as liquid for the dumplings. In a bowl, mix the butter and flour to a consistency that is slightly thicker than biscuit dough. On a floured board, roll out four circles of dough, each about 12 inches (30.5 centimeters) in diameter and 0.25 inches (6 millimeters) thick. Cut the circles into strips about 3 inches (7.6 cm) long. Bring juice to a boil, and carefully add the dumplings, one at a time. Boil slowly for about 15 minutes. Cook until dumplings are tender. Ladle into bowls. Serves five to seven.

and a wraparound buckskin skirt that extended from the waist to the knees or lower. The skirt was tied with a belt, often decorated with wampum or snakeskin. Moccasins, which had ankle flaps, were sometimes made of moose hide. Nearly all the clothing was made of buckskin—except for turkey-feather capes and fur robes worn by both men and women in cold winter months. The turkey feathers were occasionally painted, and the fur robes could be made from bear, raccoon, beaver, or other pelts sewn together. During the winter, people also wore buckskin leggings and snowshoes.

Women often decorated buckskin clothing with paintings. They sewed wampum beads into the garment or fringed it with wampum tassels. They adorned themselves with headbands, waistbands, and bandolier belts decorated with wampum. The bandolier belt was a wide, completely beaded shoulder strap attached to a beaded bag.

Both men and women liked to wear jewelry as well. This included necklaces made of long strings of wampum, copper, or red-dyed hair. The Delaware also favored metal rings and strings of wampum as earrings and bracelets. They sometimes wore porcupine quills through their noses.

Men wore snakeskins, feathers, or a circular crown of upright feathers on their heads, or sometimes a wide strip of dyed buckskin. Around their necks they hung tobacco pouches made from a whole animal skin for carrying their pipes and other small objects.

Some men, possibly warriors, shaved their heads except for a scalp lock left on the crown. Otherwise

A Delaware woman wears traditional clothes.

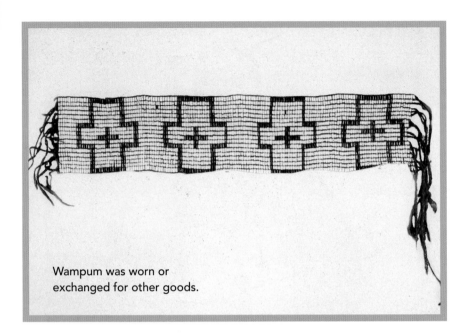

Wampum was worn or exchanged for other goods.

they wore their hair long and loose, with wampum braided or tied in as a decoration. Women usually braided their hair, perhaps in four braids sometimes tied and covered with a square pouch decorated with wampum. People often slathered their hair and skin with bear grease as protection against insects and the cold. They painted their faces and tattooed their bodies with elaborate designs.

When the Delaware started trading for cloth, women began to make most garments from this woven material, although people still preferred to wear buckskin moccasins. Today, at dances and ceremonies people still wear traditional clothing that recalls their proud heritage.

Arts and Crafts

Traditionally, the Delaware made, or traded for, all the objects they needed to survive in the forests and fields. Both men and women became skilled **artisans**, although they practiced different handicrafts. Men concentrated on making weapons and tools, skillfully chipping, or knapping, stones to make arrowheads, knives, and axes in many sizes and shapes. They made dugout canoes from the trunks of trees—probably cedar, which resisted decay—painstakingly chopping and burning the wood away. They also crafted light, small canoes from sheets of elm and other bark, and they carved wooden paddles. Additionally, they made small objects, such as pipes, from clay, stone, horn, or copper.

Delaware women had many responsibilities. Along with raising children, tending crops, gathering food and firewood, and cooking meals, they tanned animal hides, sewed clothing, and worked hard at many useful crafts. Tanning hides into soft buckskin was one of their hardest yet most important tasks.

Women made beautiful pottery for cooking and storage in many shapes and sizes. One Delaware pot found in New Jersey was large enough for two whole deer to be cooked in it. Cooking pots usually had rounded bottoms, which were held upright by three stones. A fire was built around them. Delaware pottery is remarkable because women did not use a wheel but formed perfectly shaped pots by hand. They also did not have kilns; they hardened the clay of the finished pots by firing them aboveground or in shallow pits. Later, the Delaware traded for metal pots and iron kettles.

Expert weavers, women made many kinds of baskets for storing food and belongings. These useful baskets were often decorated with painted spruce roots or porcupine quills. Women also wove mats and baskets from rushes and cornhusks. They made string, cord, and rope from plant fibers, including hemp, nettle plants, and the inner bark of certain kinds of trees. They then wove these cords into bags and fishnets.

They carved wooden bowls, dishes, and ladles. They used gourds for water bottles and often ate off leaves and shells. They fashioned mortars for grinding corn by hollowing out a stump or a section of a tree trunk. They used a heavy stick as a pestle. Sometimes they also ground corn with stones. The Delaware made small, handy objects, such as sewing needles from animal or fish bones, pine candles, and reed flutes. They made wampum from various shells—purple beads from quahogs and white beads from whelks. Strings of these wampum beads were highly valued in ceremonies, trade, and as adornments.

All of this changed in the nineteenth century, however, when the Delaware signed numerous misleading treaties that forced them to leave their homeland and travel west to Oklahoma, Wisconsin, and Canada. As a result of abandoning their homes, some of their heritage and traditions were also lost. Popular crafts such as making clay pots and chipping arrowheads and knife blades became difficult or impossible to remember. Women neglected making intricate clothing and other objects with porcupine quills, and thus the art became lost to them over time. Everyday tasks such as fishing and hunting adapted to the environment to which they relocated. The skills they had applied while living on the East Coast were lost

The People and Culture of the Delaware

Delaware women made beautiful designs using porcupine quills and beads.

to them. Worse, traditional songs and dances became difficult to remember, many tribes having merged with others in the new area. Nevertheless, some knowledge about these activities remained, ensuring that part of the Delaware's past continued with the tribe. In more recent times, people have started to work together to fully restore Delaware history, culture, and practices.

The land of the Delaware people was full of rolling hills and forests.

CHAPTER FOUR

The Delawares say, that the heavens are inhabited by men, and that the Indians descended from them to inhabit the earth.

—George Henry Loskiel, 1794

BELIEFS OF THE DELAWARE

E ach Native American group had different religious beliefs. Most believed in many gods and developed their own creation stories and myths involving them. The Delaware also had their own religious beliefs and traditions. Some of these were similar to other Native tribes, while others were unique to their specific nation.

Shamans used rattles and drums in rituals

Religion

The Delaware believed in one god, who was the creator of the universe. He was known as **Kishëlmukòng**, or He Who Creates Us by His Thoughts. They thought that the universe itself was composed of twelve layers, with the earth at the bottom and the home of the Creator at the top. Life in this heavenly twelfth realm resembled earthly life but without pain, sorrow, disease, or work. Traditionally, the number twelve had great significance to the Delaware. Not only were there twelve realms of the universe, but it took twelve days for the spirit of the deceased to reach the Creator. It also required twelve days to complete their most important ritual, the Big House Ceremony. The Delaware further believed that they had to shout twelve times before their prayers reached the Creator.

The Delaware believed that along with Kishëlmukòng, who ruled over heaven and earth, all objects, both animate and inanimate, had spirits that could bring either good or evil. The good spirits, known as *manëtuwàk*, had many roles. Somewhat similar to angels, they often served as guardian spirits for people.

The **Mësingw**, or Living Solid Face, was the guardian spirit of deer, bears, and other game animals. He helped hunters locate the game and might even be seen riding on the back of a deer. The Mësingw's face was half red and half black. The **Mësinghhòlikàn**, or dancers who portrayed him at ceremonies, dressed in bearskin regalia. Mësingw had such a fearsome reputation that parents simply mentioned his name, hinting that the spirit would get them, and children immediately behaved themselves. The image of Mësingw is today featured on the official seal of the Delaware Tribe of Indians in Oklahoma.

Conversions

After they came into contact with Europeans, the Delaware struggled against attempts at conversion by Christian missionaries. As early as the 1600s, Swedish Lutherans tried with little or no success to convert them. Later, David Brainerd, a Presbyterian, briefly sought converts, but he mostly spread consumption, a disease now known as tuberculosis. Beginning about 1740 near Bethlehem, Pennsylvania, Moravian missionaries from Germany began to work among the Delaware. As the Delaware moved west the missionaries went with them. Moravian converts were occasionally mentioned as the "Christian Indians" in Delaware treaties with

Many missionaries, including David Zeisberger, preached to the Delaware people.

the United States. The Moravians persevered in their religious efforts, but the strict nature of their beliefs discouraged many possible converts. These zealous missionaries did undertake some good works, however, including the preservation of the Northern Unami dialect, which today survives in a grammar text and dictionary prepared by the Moravian missionary David Zeisberger. They taught the Delaware how to read and write Lenape, enabling the Delaware to have their own literature.

After the Delaware went to Kansas, Methodists and Baptists preached to them, but the Delaware resisted because conversion required them to abandon the old ways. Missionary efforts tended to divide people and eventually eroded traditional beliefs. Many Delaware were drawn to these new beliefs but did not want to give up Native ways and accept Christianity as their only religion. Ultimately, despite the best intentions, many of these efforts tended to do more harm than good.

Traditional Celebrations

Traditionally, after the crops were harvested and the largest numbers of people were gathered in the villages, the Delaware held their most important ceremonies of the year. The major thanksgiving ritual was **Gamwing**, or the Big House Ceremony, which included dancing, feasting, and storytelling in a large structure known as the **Xingwikaon**, or Big House. At this celebration, people prayed for bountiful hunting. They honored the spirit Mësingw, who protected the forest animals that would be hunted through the late autumn and winter. Masks symbolizing his face were carved into living trees, then removed to be worn at various ceremonies throughout the year. People also carved small wooden masks to wear as amulets on necklaces.

They often gathered for these rituals during the day, but as the sun set, the Delaware brought the fire into the dance ground. People sat there visiting until the deep sound of the steady beat of a water drum resonated in the night, followed by the singing of the drummer. On either side of the drummer sat other singers, who shook gourd rattles and called for the women to come out and dance.

Drums were important instruments used in rituals and to play music.

Music centered on the water drum, which was made from a small hollowed log with a little water poured into the bottom and a deer hide stretched over the top. Today, the Delaware still use water drums, but they are now made from cast-iron kettles. Along with the water drum, the other musical instruments were rattles made of gourds, bark, horns, and turtle shells. However, turtle-shell rattles were usually used in sacred ceremonies, not social dances.

Like other eastern tribes, the Delaware had many songs that accompanied the water drum, which emphasized rhythm more than words. Some songs took their names from the Bean Dance or Corn Dance. Others were named after animals, as in the Raccoon Dance and Duck Dance. The Alligator Dance spread as far north as present-day New York and Canada, although this animal did not live in these locales. Most likely, the dance was brought north by one of the southeastern tribes.

More recent dances include the Stirrup Dance, in which a man dances with a woman partner. At one point in the dance, the man raises his foot and the woman places her foot on top, as if in a stirrup, and they hop as they dance. Another curious dance is the Go Get 'Em Dance, in which the women gather in front of the men and sing along with them. After about four songs the men step in, and each man chooses a woman with whom to dance around the fire.

Many of these dances and songs went west as the Delaware and other tribes were forced from their original territory. Some of the dances, such as the Duck Dance, spread widely among many tribes. However, religious or ceremonial songs and dances were rarely adopted between tribes. A few dances, such as the Cherokee Dance, were named for other tribes, although curiously the Cherokee Dance was not known to the Cherokee themselves. On some occasions the dances were given to other tribes. For instance, the Caddo shared the Turkey Dance with the Delaware and Shawnee. Since this is not a dance of eastern origin, the dancers move in a clockwise direction. By contrast, most of the dances in which the Caddo move counterclockwise were probably learned from the Delaware and Shawnee while the three tribes were living together in Texas during the nineteenth century.

As recently as 1927, the Quapaw gave the Quapaw Dance to the Delaware and Shawnee. Sometimes

Today, the Delaware celebrate many ancestral traditions at powwows.

The People and Culture of the Delaware

dances are given to another tribe to "keep" as their own. At a recent conference in Muncey, Ontario, a Munsee Delaware woman explained how her people had given the Delaware "Skin Beating Song" to the Oneida, an Iroquois tribe, since the Oneida were losing their singers. Similarly, a Cayuga man from Canada visited the Delaware while they were still in Kansas, sometime before 1867. He returned home with the Stirrup Dance, which has since been renamed the Chicken Dance or One-Side Male Dance.

The Delaware had many other songs for various sacred ceremonies—war dances, activities around the home, and, more recently, rituals of the Native American Church. Over the years, missionaries working among the Delaware have translated nearly a thousand religious hymns into the Lenape language.

Today, the Delaware people wear traditional clothing at powwows, which include Stomp Dances that are held throughout the year. These are not religious gatherings but largely popular social gatherings in which people love to dance to the beat and songs of a drum group.

Well-Being and Illness

The first European explorers and colonists were impressed by the lack of illness and infirmities among the Delaware. From an early age, the Delaware sought good health. Each day for several months they plunged newborn babies into cold water or snow. To purify their bodies and their spirits, men and women visited the sweat lodge every day. They poured water over heated stones to fill the hut with steam. After sweating

Corn was an important crop to many Delaware tribes.

for a half hour or so, they dove into the cold water of a nearby stream to clean the open pores of their skin.

In times of illness they relied on the **shaman**, or doctor, called **mëteìnu**, who could be either a man or a woman. These healers had an excellent knowledge of herbal medicine, which they applied skillfully. They handled plants with great respect and even sought to speak with their spirits. Certain plants, such as corn, were believed to nourish the soul as well as the body. Their many cures included walnut sap, which soothed inflammation; jimsonweed, which was applied to burns; ironweed, which helped facial blemishes; tea from elderberry leaves, which eased colic; sassafras, which reduced high blood pressure; and even poison ivy roots, which were crushed, roasted, and applied as a poultice.

The Delaware believed that illness, injuries, and even death were caused by evil spirits in the body, the patient's wrongful behavior, or an encounter with an apparition. If people failed to obey the laws of nature, they believed that illness or other misfortune would befall them. Most people carried medicine bundles, small buckskin pouches in which they kept dried plants, roots, feathers, stones, and other sacred objects. They thought that these objects would help to ward off bad luck. They also observed special practices, such as refraining from eating certain foods. If a person became very sick, a powerful doctor would be asked to perform healing rituals.

Telling Stories

Among the Delaware, the storyteller occupied an honored place. Historian, teacher, and entertainer, the storyteller kept alive the customs and beliefs of the people. Most often, people gathered around the fire to listen to stories in the winter, when there was not as much work to be done. Some stories included songs. Several examples are known from the Unami Delaware. Here is one that used to be told (and sung) by the Munsee to entertain young children. Notice the mischievous suggestion that the neighbors might have eaten the woman's little boy.

> They say there was once a foolish woman,
> and she had a little boy. She left him by
> himself. When she came back, he was nowhere.
> She looked in the neighbor's cooking fire.
> Then she found his tracks leading to a tree.
> He was singing.

"Pitiful
Pitiful
All alone
It seems
I'll be a quail
Potchpai [call of the quail]."

As he finished his song, one arm fell out of the tree. He sang again, and a leg fell down. Again, and his head fell. All of him fell. Each time, "Potchpai."

That is why the Delaware always hated to kill quail: they are that woman's little boy. It is why I tell the story. It is an ancient one.

Fun and Play

The Delaware enjoyed many kinds of games, including *pahsahëman*, the Lenape version of football. Although it is called football, the Delaware game is very different from the popular American sport. Historically, several different versions of pahsahëman were played among eastern tribes. Some were men against men, but men were usually pitted against women in a rough-and-tumble contest. The Delaware may have learned the game from the Shawnee, who moved into the homeland of the Delaware in eastern Pennsylvania around 1692, but they may have been playing the game as early as 1656.

The Delaware brought the game to Oklahoma in the late 1800s. They used a soft, oblong ball called *pahsahikàn*. Made of buckskin stuffed with deer hair, it is about the size of a softball. Players competed on a field about 100 yards (91 m) long with goalposts, made of branches, at each end. The goalposts were about 15 feet (4.6 m) high and set about 6 feet (1.8 m) apart. Players had to get the ball through the goalposts to score a point, and traditionally it took just one score to win the game. Today, when the Oklahoma Delaware play this game, they tally the score to twelve points.

Games usually began in the afternoon. To start, a man tossed the ball up among the players in the center of the field. A man could catch the ball, but he was not allowed to throw or carry it. He had to pass by kicking the ball as the women grabbed him. If a man caught or intercepted the ball, he had to stand there and kick it toward the men's goal or toward another man. A man could not tackle or grab a woman who had the ball, but could only block her passes or knock the ball from her hands. Female players could carry, pass, or even kick the ball to another player or through the goalposts.

A pile of twelve sticks, each about 2 inches (5 cm) long, was used to keep score. The sticks were put in two rows, one for men and one for women. Whichever team earned twelve sticks, or the most sticks at the end of the game, was the winner. If the women were losing a game, one of their favorite tricks was to give the ball to a frail old woman, who was often helped through the goalposts with the ball by some of the younger women. They knew that the men would not try to knock the ball from that old woman's hands.

Usually, the Delaware began to play football in the spring, when the weather grew warm, and continued until about mid-June. No set number of games was

Pottery made by Moravian Delaware tribe members

played during the season. People simply competed until they got tired. Before the first game of the year, an elder offered a prayer, thanking the Creator for allowing the people to play again and asking that he might let them live to play in future years. At the end of the last game in June, a female elder offered a prayer as she broke open the ball and let the deer hair fall to the ground. The hide was then made into another ball for the next spring.

Besides football, the Delaware enjoyed many other games, including the *kokolësh*, or rabbit tail game. The object of the game was to catch cones on a pointed stick to which a rabbit tail had been tied. In *selahtikàn*, pieces of reed decorated with various lines and dots

The People and Culture of the Delaware

indicating their value in points were dropped onto a surface and then picked up one at a time without moving the others. In *mamandin*, dice made of painted bone or deer antler were placed in a wooden bowl. A player then struck the bowl down against a folded hide or blanket hard enough to make the dice jump in the bowl. The score was determined by the colors that turned up.

In Canada, where some Delaware people were forced to migrate years ago, people learned to play a game called snow snake. In this game, players threw a long pole like a spear along an icy trough in the snow. Sometimes, people splashed water along the trench prior to the contest so that it was glazed with ice. The object was to see who could throw their spear the farthest down the trench or over the ice.

Throughout the years, the Delaware's presence continues to be felt and experienced by many. Traditional games and powwows are celebrated throughout the United States, particularly in Oklahoma. By participating in such events, people connect to the history and heritage of the Delaware.

Many early Native Americans lived in longhouses near rivers.

CHAPTER
FIVE

*Success is only a
measure of how far
we bounce, after we
hit bottom.*

—Chief Chet Brooks,
Delaware Indian News
April 2015

OVERCOMING HARDSHIPS

As centuries passed and the Delaware settled in the eastern part of what would become the United States, their world began to change, at first subtly but then in very noticeable ways. This was particularly due to the presence of Europeans, who traveled overseas to colonize America in the 1600s. After their arrival, the Delaware's lives would never be the same.

Relations with the Europeans

When the first Europeans landed in Delaware territory, the Native people were curious. These were new people they had never before seen, arriving with objects only ever imagined. Who were they? What did they want? It soon became clear that these newcomers would only bring sadness and turmoil.

At first, the Delaware tried to get along with European colonists, but they were soon asked to sign treaties in which they surrendered their land. Open conflict between the Delaware and the Dutch intensified in 1638, after Governor William Kieft assumed authority over New Netherland (present-day New York). To help with the cost of building forts to protect the Dutch against Native Americans and English colonists, who also wanted control of Delaware land, he made the Delaware pay a tax in the form of corn, furs, and wampum. The Delaware did not take kindly to this act. They believed they were being unjustly punished, and protested. On February 25, 1643, Kieft sent a force of soldiers to a Delaware village to demand payment. However, the soldiers brutally massacred 120 people, including children and the elderly. The Delaware responded by burning Dutch houses and farm buildings and destroying cattle and corn. Years of hostility followed, escalating into a two-year conflict known as the Peach War. This war was triggered when a Delaware woman was shot and killed for picking peaches on land claimed by a Dutchman. In retaliation, two hundred warriors attacked New Netherland, killing at least fifty Dutch colonists. Conflicts continued into the 1660s in what came to be called the Esopus Wars, as the Dutch attempted to push on to Native American lands on the west bank of the Hudson River.

Meanwhile, many English settlers were moving into New Netherland. In 1664, the Dutch colony was seized by an English fleet and subsequently renamed New York. Instead of fighting Native warriors, the English decided to take hostile individuals to court, thus entangling them in confusing contracts and legal claims. Many Delaware moved to Pennsylvania, where they sought refuge among the Quakers. William Penn, the Quaker founder of this colony, advocated fair and peaceful relations with Native people, and the Quakers were more friendly toward Native Americans. Penn believed that colonists could live in harmony with the Delaware and other tribes if they were accepted as equals. Several Delaware chiefs, notably Tammany, made a peace treaty with Penn in 1682, which brought about goodwill for nearly half a century. Penn admired the Delaware for their generosity. He even believed they might be descendants of one of the lost tribes of Israel.

Yet ultimately the Penn family deceived and took advantage of the Delaware in the outrageously unjust agreement that came to be known as the Walking Purchase. In 1686, Delaware leaders had agreed to an unsigned deed in which they were to surrender as much of their land as a man could walk in a day and a half. In 1737, Thomas Penn, son of William Penn; James Logan, provincial secretary; and other colonial officials pressured the Delaware to have the deed to this land transferred to the Penn family. Then they schemed to claim an immense swath of the territory—much of the Delaware lands in eastern Pennsylvania.

This illustration displays the Walking Purchase, where the Delaware lost much of their land to Thomas Penn.

The Delaware were led to believe that a man would steadily pace the distance, resting along the way, and thereby claim a reasonably sized tract of land. However, Penn hired a crew of axmen to clear an easy path through the forest for three fast, strong runners. Beginning at the forks of the Lehigh and Delaware Rivers, the three men ran 30 miles (48.2 km) in just

The People and Culture of the Delaware

six hours, after which two of them dropped out. However, the third man, Edward Marshall, rested for a few hours and then resumed a swift journey of 66.5 miles (107 km) across the Kittatinny Ridge and into the Pocono Mountains.

Penn then demanded that the boundary run at a right angle to the Delaware River, to include even more land. Through this monstrous deceit the Penns were able to steal 1,200 square miles (3,108 square kilometers) of territory from the Delaware. Lappawinsoe and other tribal chiefs accused Pennsylvania officials of fraud. However, colonial officials then prevailed upon the Iroquois to drive the Delaware from their land. Because of this deception, many Delaware warriors chose to side with the French against the British in the French and Indian War (1754–1763).

Following the Walking Purchase of 1737, the Delaware splintered into various groups and bands as they were repeatedly driven from one place to another by encroaching settlers. Most people migrated to eastern Ohio, where they established villages and prosperous farms along the Muskingum River. Others gathered in small settlements around Pittsburgh and northwestern Ohio. On September 17, 1778, the Delaware signed their first treaty with the newly formed

Many Delaware people converted to Christianity after the arrival of Europeans.

United States government. Nevertheless, through war and peace they had to continue to surrender their lands and move westward—first to Ohio, then to Indiana, Missouri, Kansas, and finally to **Indian Territory** in what is now Oklahoma.

Evolving Times

Many of those who settled in Pennsylvania were converted by the Moravians, a religious group that had established missions in Bethlehem, Pennsylvania, and elsewhere in Delaware territory. In 1782, the Gnadenhütten mission in Ohio was mercilessly attacked by frontiersmen in revenge for raids on

The People and Culture of the Delaware

their settlements. Although the peaceful Delaware of the mission had not participated in any hostilities, about a hundred of them were massacred. To escape further persecution, many of the surviving Munsee-speaking Delaware fled to the province of Ontario, in Canada, where they established Moraviantown along the Thames River. Later, during the War of 1812, this village was attacked by American soldiers.

By the end of the 1700s, most of the Unami-speaking bands had migrated from Ohio to Indiana to escape intensifying hostilities with American settlers. Those who remained were badly defeated, along with warriors from other tribes, in the Battle of Fallen Timbers. In the 1795 Treaty of Greenville, the Delaware and other Native peoples in the Old Northwest—present-day Ohio, Indiana, Illinois, Wisconsin, and Michigan—were forced to surrender their land once again and relocate farther west. In 1829, the federal government established a Delaware reservation in the northern part of Indian Territory, in eastern Kansas. As part of the **Indian Removal Act** of 1830, all Native Americans were required to move west of the Mississippi. While the main group moved to Kansas, a number of Unami-speaking people decided to join the Caddo, a tribe living in Texas. However, in 1859 these people, along with the Caddo, were forced to move to Anadarko in western Oklahoma, where the Unami eventually came to be recognized as the Delaware Nation. In 1866, those who had moved to Kansas were required to sign yet another treaty, surrendering their land and agreeing to join the Cherokee in eastern Oklahoma. In 1890 they were recognized as Cherokee citizens. These "Cherokee

Delaware" lost most of their land as a result of the General **Allotment** Act of 1887 yet continued to maintain a strong presence in eastern Oklahoma.

A small group later known as the Sand Hill Delaware remained in Monmouth County, New Jersey. Composed of Delaware, Cherokee, and people of European descent, they supported themselves as carpenters and craftsmen in a community that came to be called Neptune. The settlement gradually became a center for Native American religious ceremonies and social events, such as powwows. After 1890, the people began to leave the community, and although the Sand Hill group continued to be recognized through the twentieth and twenty-first centuries, its members were widely dispersed.

Other Delaware found homes in Ontario. Some scattered to Wisconsin, and during the Great Depression of the 1930s, many who had lived in Oklahoma migrated to California. Wherever they lived, Delaware people struggled to maintain their culture and identity, often against great odds.

Preserving the Language

The Delaware spoke dialects of two closely related languages in the Algonquian family of languages: Munsee and Unami. These two, together with Mahican, form a subfamily called Delawaran. Nevertheless, Mahican, formerly spoken in the upper Hudson Valley just north of Munsee territory, is quite distinct from either Munsee or Unami. Even more distinct are the other Algonquian languages of the eastern seaboard, such as Nanticoke, formerly spoken

After the Delaware were forced from their homeland, they scattered across America. Some Delaware tribes came to live with the Cherokee (pictured here).

Overcoming Hardships

to the south and west of the Unami, and the various languages of New England, spoken in the region just east and south of the Munsee. These languages, however, all shared many words and grammatical features. As mentioned, the language survived partly because of missionaries' efforts to preserve the Delaware language and teach the people how to read and write in their Native dialect.

The Delaware believe that at one time all the Algonquian-speaking peoples were one tribe, which grew and dispersed in different directions. As they lived apart, their languages became more distinctive.

The following words and phrases are Unami, drawn from the *Lenape Language Lessons* by Nora Thompson Dean of the Delaware Tribe of Indians in eastern Oklahoma. The language is complex, but the following key will help in pronunciation.

a as in father
à as in up
e as in gate
è as in get
ë as in sofa
i as in me
ì as in pick
o as in open
ò as in for
u as in boot
ù as in pull
x as in the German nacht

The People and Culture of the Delaware

The stress in Unami Delaware usually falls on the next-to-last syllable. When it falls on any other, the vowel that is stressed is underlined.

Common Words and Phrases

hè	Hello! (or) Hi!
kshàxën	It is windy.
kùmhòkòt	It is cloudy.
làpìch knewël	I will see you again. (good-bye)
lëlëwàxën	There is a breeze.
lëm<u>a</u>tahpi	Sit down!
mitsi	Eat! (speaking to one person)
mitsikw	You eat! (speaking to two or more)
mitsitàm	Let's eat!
mushhakòt	The sky is clear.
ngatungòm	I am sleepy.
ngatupwi	I am hungry.
ngat<u>u</u>sëmwi	I am thirsty.
pèthakhòn	It is thundering.
shëlànde	It is a hot day.
s<u>u</u>këlan	It is raining.
taktani	I don't know.
tëmike	Come in! (or) Go in!
tuk<u>i</u>hëla	Wake up!
wëli kishku	It is a good day.

wëndaxa	Come here!
wine	It is snowing.

Animals

ahas	crow
chingwe	bobcat
chulëns	bird
dalëmuns	my pet
òkwës	fox
pukwès	mouse
sàngwe	weasel
xanikw	squirrel

Numbers

kwëti	one
nisha	two
naxa	three
newa	four
palenàxk	five
kwëtash	six
nishash	seven
xash	eight
pèshkung	nine
tèlën	ten

Many young people continue to celebrate the traditions of their tribe.

While the Delaware faced many hardships and difficulties, they persevered and remained a part of Native American culture. Their existence was not always easy, but with each difficulty faced, they became stronger and more determined to survive.

Members of the Delaware Tribe
participate in a powwow.

The People and Culture of the Delaware

It is up to the next generation to continue studying and commemorating the history of the Delaware.

*We are in a time of
renewal, and a time
of great change.*

—lenapenation.org

THE NATION'S PRESENCE NOW

The Delaware continue to exist today. While separated from their initial homelands, they have established successful communities in various parts of the Midwest. They continue to be involved in Native events and are proud of their heritage.

A Migrating Tribe

In the early 1800s, when many Delaware were living in Indiana, the group that eventually settled in western Oklahoma split off and migrated through Arkansas and into Texas. Driven out of Texas in 1859, these Absentee Delaware, as they were then called, at last found their permanent home near Anadarko, Oklahoma, where they became known as the Delaware Tribe of Western Oklahoma and finally, as of 2000, simply the Delaware Nation. After leaving Indiana, the main Delaware tribe went to Kansas, where they lived for about thirty years until they were forced to move into Indian Territory in present-day eastern Oklahoma. Therefore, two Delaware groups live in Oklahoma today: the Delaware Nation at Anadarko and the Delaware Tribe of Indians, headquartered in Bartlesville, Oklahoma.

With around 1,400 members, the Delaware Nation— formerly the Delaware Tribe of Western Oklahoma— jointly owns 487 acres (197 hectares) of trust land in Caddo County, Oklahoma, with the Wichita and Caddo tribes. Under the Indian Reorganization Act of 1934 these people suffered because they had not been counted as Delaware in any census from 1895 to 1930. Finally they were organized under the Oklahoma Indian Welfare Act of 1936, and they began the long struggle to rebuild their cultural identity.

Today, the Delaware Nation does many things to ensure its culture is preserved. For example, it has a detailed website, www.delawarenation.com, that features information about the tribe. The website offers Lenape language classes, in addition to communal activities and events. The nation is likewise committed to preserving geographical and historical sites important to them, and is involved in several funding,

The Collect Pond was once a source of water for early
Lenape/Delaware people.

educational, and caretaker programs. They are likewise advocates for the use of solar energy and are finding ways to include solar power into their reservation.

The Delaware Nation operates under its own constitution and bylaws, passed in 1973. A tribal headquarters is located about 2 miles (3.2 km) north of Anadarko, Oklahoma, which is about 50 miles (80.4 km) southwest of Oklahoma City. Composed of a president, vice president, secretary, treasurer, and two committee members, an executive committee serves as the elected governing body. Members serve staggered four-year terms. Tribal leaders are working to improve the quality of life of tribal members and to restore traditional culture. They maintain a community center and also a senior citizens center for tribal elders. Artifacts are preserved in a tribal museum and a library. The tribe also participates in the Four Tribes Consortium of Oklahoma, which provides tribal members with vocational training and jobs.

The much larger Delaware Tribe of Indians has about eleven thousand members, many of whom live in Washington, Nowata, Craig, and Delaware counties, Oklahoma. In 1996, leaders successfully sought recognition as a tribe separate from the Cherokee of Oklahoma. They are governed by the Tribal Business Committee. The tribe has a headquarters, gift shop, and community and child development building in Bartlesville, as well as another in Caney, Kansas, where they purchased land in 2013. Additionally, they have an active website and social media presence. Their website, delawaretribe.org, offers information about the tribe, ways to connect to the tribe, and enrollment

The Delaware tribes first settled in areas with abundant water and land.

forms for those who are eligible to join the tribe. Their Facebook page is up-to-date with information about the tribe, other Native people in the area, and tribal news and upcoming events. They likewise have a cultural center and promote preserving nature and celebrating and taking care of the elderly.

In an effort to re-establish themselves, the Delaware Tribe of Indians adopted a new tribal seal in January 2013. After forty years of their previous seal, the new seal sought to more accurately portray the Delaware as a nation. It reconfigured traditional Delaware symbols, such as a wolf's print, a turtle, and a turkey talon. Meanwhile, an image of the Plains peace pipe, which had no connection to the Delaware's rituals, was removed. The name on the seal was also changed from "Lenni Lenape" to simply "Lenape," which means "The People."

During the 1950s, the two Oklahoma tribes jointly sought claims with the Indian Claims Commission. In

This sign welcomes people to the Stockbridge-Munsee Reservation. Here, Munsee Delaware people live alongside the Mohicans.

STOCKBRIDGE MUNSEE
Band of Mohican Indians

Mohican
Nation

the 1960s, the commission awarded more than $12 million to the Delaware in Oklahoma. There followed a long period of litigation, but on February 23, 1977, the US Supreme Court finally released these funds, along with interest. Ten percent was set aside for tribal use, and the rest was divided among tribal members.

Established in 1856, the Stockbridge-Munsee Reservation in Shawano County, Wisconsin, consists of about 22,000 acres (8,900 ha). Of Mohican and Munsee ancestry, the Stockbridge-Munsee population in 2015 was about 750 on or near the reservation, with about 1,500 total people enrolled as members. A seven-member elected council governs the tribe. The tribe does much to promote its heritage. It has its own website, www.mohican-nsn.gov, and updates it regularly with information about reservation activity.

In Ontario the Munsee Delaware survive mainly in two communities: the Delaware Nation at Moraviantown and the Munsee Delaware Nation (located in Muncey, Ontario). There are over 1,000 members of the Moraivantown band, with 550 residents living on the reservation. The band has an active social media presence and an up-to-date website, delawarenation.on.ca, that discusses the reservation's activity. The Munsee Delaware Nation, on the other hand, has a population of about 600, a third of whom live on the reservation. As of 2015, their land covered 2,604 acres (1,054 ha), but they were working toward sanctioning a land claim that would gain more territory. They too have an online community, www.munseedelawarenation.org, and an active Facebook page.

In the 1980s and 1990s, the New Jersey legislature finally recognized several groups of mixed ancestry, including the Powhatan-Renápe Nation, the Ramapough Mountain Indians, and the Nanticoke Lenni Lenape Indians. These groups are federally recognized tribes that receive funding and support from the government.

Cultural Connections

Since the 1960s, various Delaware communities have been actively engaged in cultural programs to preserve language, music, and dance. Naming ceremonies continue to be held, although they may not have the same religious significance as in the past. Nora Thompson Dean, a tribal member who died in 1984, was especially active in maintaining traditional ways and passing her knowledge on to others. Today, many Delaware tribes offer resources that aim to educate others about their tribe and help preserve their culture. Some of the Delaware tribe websites offer brief language introductions, while others offer language lessons to their communities. Moreover, since 1992 the Moraviantown Delaware has hosted an annual gathering for Delaware people from all over North America, with feasting, drumming, and singing just as in the old-time Delaware Big House Ceremony.

Today, people from all over the world take an interest in Native American history and the history of the Delaware. People come together each year to learn from the Delaware, observe their powwows and ceremonies, and witness their culture being practiced and passed down from one generation to the next.

Dancing is an important part of Delaware culture and history.

The Nation's Presence Now

A Delaware man named Enoch wears clothing for which he had traded, circa 1870.

*The name [Tammany]
is held in the highest
veneration among
[the Lenape].*

—Reverend John
Heckewelder, 1876

FACES OF THE DELAWARE NATION

Throughout history, many men, women, and children have called the Delaware Nation their tribe. Some people have earned a permanent place in the tribe's history. These are a few of the men and women who have influenced the tribe or asserted their name firmly within the Delaware culture.

Black Beaver (Sucktum Mahway, Sekettu Maquah) (circa 1806–1880), trapper, trader, interpreter, scout, was born in Illinois. When he grew up, he traveled west to the Rocky Mountains, where he became a fur trapper and trader. In 1834, he and Jesse Chisholm became interpreters for an expedition led by General Henry Leavenworth and Colonel Henry Dodge to explore the Red River territory of the Comanche, Kiowa, and Wichita peoples. During the Mexican War of 1846 he became an army scout for General William Selby Harney. In the California gold rush of 1849, Black Beaver and Captain Randolph Marcy led a wagon train of five hundred people through the arid Southwest. As he returned east, Black Beaver blazed a new trail from the Brazos River in what is now northwest Texas to Fort Smith, Arkansas. He worked as a trader during the 1850s then became a Union scout during the Civil War (1861–1865). He and Jesse Chisholm served as interpreters for Southern Plains tribes at the Little Arkansas Council in 1865. In later years, Black Beaver became a representative for the Delaware people in negotiations with federal officials. He died in Anadarko, Oklahoma, near the Washita River.

James Bouchard (Watomika, Swift Foot) (1823–1889), Catholic priest, public speaker, was the son of Chief Kistalwa and his wife, Monotowa, a French woman who had been captured and raised by the Comanche. Not long after his father was killed by Sioux warriors in 1834, Bouchard converted to the Presbyterian religion and went to a mission school in Ohio. In 1846 he converted to Catholicism and began studies in Missouri to become

a Jesuit priest. In 1855, he became the first Native American in the United States to be ordained a Catholic priest. In 1861, he became a missionary to miners living in San Francisco. Father Bouchard also offered lectures on his experiences as a Native American and a Christian.

Buckongahelas (Buckangehela, Breaker of Pieces) (died ca. 1804), leader, was band chief of the Delaware living along the Miami and White Rivers in Ohio. During the American Revolution (1775–1783) he fought on the side of the British. During the 1790s he again led Delaware warriors against the Americans in Little Turtle's War, in alliance with the Miami, led by Little Turtle, and the Shawnee, led by Blue Jacket. The tribes attempted unsuccessfully to drive American settlers from their territory in the Old Northwest. After their defeat at the Battle of Fallen Timbers in August 1794, Buckongahelas was outraged that the British would not shelter the fleeing warriors at Fort Miami. Forced to accept peace with the United States, he signed the Greenville Treaty of 1795, the Fort Wayne Treaty of 1803, and the Vincennes Treaty of 1804.

Nora Thompson Dean

Nora Thompson Dean was an iconic member of the Delaware Nation.

(Weènjipahkihëlèxkwe, Touching Leaves) (1907–1984), author, lecturer, and name giver, was the best-known Delaware traditionalist of her generation. A fluent speaker of Unami Delaware, she attended the last complete performance of the Big House Ceremony in 1924, and in her later years, she became an authority on Delaware oral history and religion. By many she was considered one of the last full-blooded Delaware Natives. Born in Indian Territory, she lived in Dewey, Oklahoma, just north of Bartlesville, where she received a steady stream of visiting linguists, anthropologists, and historians. Known for her generosity as well as her inexhaustible knowledge, she contributed information for more than twenty-five books and was herself the author or coauthor of a dozen publications. Between 1972 and 1981, she received awards from the governors of New Jersey, Delaware, Pennsylvania, and Oklahoma and was named an Oklahoma Ambassador of Goodwill. She died in 1984 at the age of seventy-seven.

Gelelemend (Killbuck, William Henry) (1737–1811), peace chief, was born in Pennsylvania, the son of Killbuck, a name by which Gelelemend also came to be known. In 1778 he succeeded White Eyes, and like his predecessors, he sought peace with American settlers. However, Hopocan, a leader of the war faction, successfully opposed him, and encouraged by government officials at Fort Pitt, Gelelemend and his followers moved to an island in the Allegheny River. However, in 1782 a group of settlers was returning on the river from an attack on peaceful Delaware people at a Moravian settlement at Gnadenhütten. They attacked Gelelemend's village, killing or wounding several people, and the chief had to escape by swimming away. During his flight he lost treaty documents given to the Delaware by William Penn in 1682. Gelelemend later moved to Pittsburgh to escape attacks from Delaware warriors who blamed him for attacks by settlers. He became a Moravian convert and lived there under his Christian name of William Henry until his death.

Hopocan (Hopokan, Tobacco Pipe; Captain Pipe; Konieschguanokee, Maker of Delight) (ca. 1725–1794), war chief, sided with the French in the French and Indian War (1754–1763) and he participated in Pontiac's Rebellion of 1763. He and his followers later settled along the Muskingum River in Ohio territory. During the American Revolution, Hopocan allied with the British and led many bloody raids on American settlers on the frontier. However, Hopocan was at odds with Delaware chief White Eyes, who sided with the Americans. In 1778, Gelelemend succeeded White Eyes and led a peace faction that opposed Hopocan. Although Hopocan took part in peace discussions and signed a treaty at Fort Pitt in 1778, conflicts with settlers continued. In 1782, allied warriors defeated troops led by Colonel William Crawford, who was captured and tortured by Hopocan's band. The warriors were retaliating for attacks on peaceful Natives at Moravian settlements, but Crawford happened to be a close friend of George Washington. The death of Crawford prompted Washington to intensify military campaigns against Native American people on the western frontier. Hopocan signed peace treaties with the United States in 1785 and 1787. During the American Revolution he and his band were often forced to move. Eventually, they settled in what became known as Captain Pipe's Village, along the upper Sandusky River in Ohio.

Jacobs (Captain Jacobs) (died 1756), war chief, led a band during the French and Indian War (1754–1763) against the British. In July 1755, he joined the French and other Native American warriors in attacking British and colonial troops under General Edward Braddock while Braddock was en route to attack Fort Duquesne at the site of present-day Pittsburgh. Of the two thousand soldiers, only five hundred escaped to Fort Cumberland, and Braddock himself was killed. Along with other Native American warriors, Jacobs and his band continued to raid British settlements on the frontier of western Pennsylvania. However, in September 1756 Colonel John Armstrong attacked the Delaware village of Kittanning, where Jacobs was living, and torched many of the homes. Jacobs and many of his followers, including his entire family, were killed as they tried to escape the slaughter.

Charles Journeycake (Neshapanasumin) (1817–1894), trapper, guide, preacher, leader, was born on the upper

Charles Journeycake, circa 1854

Sandusky River in Ohio. He was the son of Chief Solomon Journeycake and his Delaware-French wife. At the age of eleven, Charles had to move with his band to the northern part of Indian Territory in present-day Kansas. Baptized in 1833, he is believed to be the first Delaware person converted to Christianity west of the Mississippi River. When he became a trapper and guide, he often preached to his companions during their ventures into the West. In 1841, he became a charter member of the Delaware and Mohegan Baptist Mission Church.

In 1854, the northern part of Indian Territory became Kansas and Nebraska territories, and the Delaware were again forced to move. Now a subchief, Journeycake helped to negotiate with federal officials for a new Delaware homeland in Oklahoma. In 1867, Journeycake and his Delaware-French wife, Jane Sosha, moved onto former Cherokee land, where he worked as a farmer and pastor. He helped to found Alluwe Indian Church and Bacone College, and he translated religious writings into the Algonquian language. In the 1890s, Journeycake assisted with a successful Delaware land claim against the Cherokee and the federal government in which the Delaware were compensated for land sales in Kansas and Oklahoma.

Lappawinsoe (Gathering Provisions) (ca. 1700–unknown), leader, was one of twelve chiefs who met at Philadelphia in 1737 with Thomas Penn, son of William Penn; James Logan, provincial secretary; and other colonial officials. He and the other chiefs signed a treaty that affirmed an earlier agreement of 1686, which granted land from the

Chief Lappawinsoe

forks of the Lehigh and Delaware Rivers as far as a man could walk in a day and a half. Penn and the other officials pressured Lappawinsoe and the other tribal leaders to agree to what became known as the Walking Purchase.

Instead of slowly pacing the distance and resting along the way, the officials had a path cut through the tract and hired three swift, strong runners, who covered 30 miles (48.2 km) in just six hours. Two of them dropped out, but Edward Marshall spent a few hours at Lappawinsoe's village and then continued his fast-paced journey of 66.5 miles (107 km) across the Kittatinny Ridge and into the Pocono Mountains. Penn and Lodge then insisted that the returning line run at a right angle to the Delaware River instead of to the closest point. By this trickery, they were able to claim 1,200 square miles (3,108 sq km) of Delaware territory. Lappawinsoe and the other chiefs accused the colonial officials of fraud, but these officials called in the Iroquois, who drove the Delaware from their homeland. Because of this deception, many Delaware warriors sided with the French against the British in the French and Indian War (1754–1763).

Nemacolin (active mid-1700s), leader, worked with Thomas Cresap, a Maryland settler, to blaze a trail between the Potomac and Monongahela rivers from 1749 to 1750. Extending through the Allegheny Mountains from present-day Virginia through western Maryland and into Pennsylvania, the route became known as Nemacolin's Path. In 1752 the Ohio Company expanded the trail from Fort Cumberland, Maryland, to the Youghiogheny River, and in 1754 George Washington extended the route to Uniontown, Pennsylvania. A year later, in 1755, General Braddock traveled this route during the French and Indian War (1754–1763). His force included three hundred axmen and carpenters, who widened the road to 12 feet (3.6 m) and laid bridges over the streams. In the 1780s, Pennsylvania and Maryland improved the road to carry droves of settlers and wagons on their journey westward. The town of Nemacolin, Pennsylvania, is named after the Delaware chief.

Neolin (Delaware Prophet, The Enlightened One) (active 1760s), shaman, leader, had a religious experience in the 1760s in which he claimed to have journeyed to the spirit world. There he met the Master of Life, who presented him with a set of laws. Neolin then began to preach to the Delaware and other Native people from his home along the Cuyahoga River in the Lake Erie region of northern Ohio. He urged people to renounce all European beliefs, practices, and trade goods, especially firearms and whiskey. Neolin called upon people to return to tribal ways but to abandon magic, polygamy, and warfare among themselves. On deerskins he drew maps that illustrated the path to enlightenment, and he made prayer sticks inscribed with a daily prayer, which he left at the villages he visited.

Neolin foretold a war with the non–Native Americans, and his hostile stance appealed to many tribes in the region and to Pontiac. The great Ottawa chief strongly encouraged all the tribes to unite against settlers, although he still encouraged alliance with the French and supported the use of firearms. Many tribes allied in Pontiac's Rebellion of 1763 and nearly succeeded in defeating the British. After the alliance fell apart, Neolin went to live in Wakatomica's Shawnee village and Newcomer's Delaware village. His teachings came to influence Tenskwatawa, the Shawnee prophet and brother of Tecumseh.

Papounan (Papoonan) (unknown–1775), shaman, was a member of a Munsee band that was forced to move from the Hudson and Delaware Rivers of New York and New Jersey by the 1740s. For a while he lived with his band in the Lackawanna region of western New York and the Tioga and Wyalusing areas of north-central Pennsylvania. When his father died, Papounan went to live alone in the woods for five days. During this time he had a vision, in which he received his calling to become a shaman, or medicine man, for the Delaware. Thereafter, he urged his people to continue traditional ways and reject whiskey and rum. However, he also encouraged tolerance of Quaker and Moravian religious beliefs and peaceful relations with the French and English. His band did not take part in the French and Indian War (1754–1763) or Pontiac's Rebellion of 1763. Papounan's followers came to be known as Quaker Indians by some people. In 1763 they accepted a Moravian missionary named David Zeisberger as their religious leader. Papounan was baptized a Christian, and in the early 1770s he began to preach among the Delaware and other Native American people living around the Muskingum River in Ohio.

Tammany (Tamanend, Tamenend, Tamany) (ca. 1625–1701), leader, was an Unami who lived along the Delaware River, most likely in the area of present-day Bucks County, Pennsylvania. It is believed that he welcomed William Penn to the region in October 1682 and a year later negotiated two treaties with the English colonist at Shackamaxon, which became Philadelphia. Tammany also took part in a Delaware council with settlers in 1694 and encouraged peaceful relations. He signed a third peace treaty in 1697.

Tammany had no more power than other chiefs, but he had a strong, magnetic personality. He was also an advocate of peace, and he became highly regarded among colonists. In a legend, it is said that he once struggled for several days with an evil spirit that tried to overcome him. After his death, American colonists used his name to ridicule the British reverence for such figures as Saint George and Saint Andrew; they claimed

Tammany is remembered in this statue at Gettysburg.

an American-born "Saint" Tammany, who became the "patron saint" of various patriotic societies. After the Revolution, in 1789, a new Society of St. Tammany was formed in New York City. Informally known as Tammany Hall, it became a dominant political force, ruling New York City politics in the nineteenth century.

Tatamy (Moses Tatamy, Tunda Tatamy) (ca. 1695–ca. 1771), leader, was born on the east side of the Delaware River in what is now New Jersey. Not long after the 1737 Walking Purchase, Tatamy was given a tract of land near Stockertown, Pennsylvania, in payment for his services as an interpreter. In the 1740s, when many other Delaware people were being forced to move westward, Tatamy was granted permission by Pennsylvania officials to remain on his land. In 1745, he was baptized by a Presbyterian missionary named David Brainerd, with whom he had worked as an interpreter. Tatamy moved to New Jersey for his safety and became an interpreter during the French and Indian War (1754–1763). He was instrumental in gaining Teedyuscung's support for the English. In 1757, Tatamy's son was killed by a non–Native

American youth while accompanying Delaware leaders to a peace council in Easton, Pennsylvania. The tragedy nearly ended the negotiations, but the English vowed to bring the murderer to justice. Tatamy and his wife, Ann, had at least three children, two sons and a daughter. The town of Tatamy in Northampton County, Pennsylvania, is named for him.

Teedyuscung (Tedyuscung, Tedyuskung, Tediuscung) (1700–1763), war chief, was born near present-day Trenton, New Jersey. His father was known to the English as Old Man Harris. Around 1730, Teedyuscung migrated with his band to the upper Delaware River, in what is now eastern Pennsylvania and northern New Jersey. With Chief Lappawinsoe, he frequently accused the English of deceit in the Walking Purchase of 1737.

The deceptive taking of Delaware lands made Teedyuscung very suspicious toward colonists as he negotiated Native American support for the English and French. In 1750, he was baptized with the Christian name Gideon by Moravian missionaries at Gnadenhütten. In 1754, he departed Gnadenhütten and moved to Pasigachkunk, on the Cowanesque River. The same year, he took part in the Albany Congress, where he met William Johnson and tribal representatives of the Iroquois League.

In the early years of the French and Indian War, Teedyuscung served as a war chief of Delaware, Shawnee, and Mahican warriors and led attacks on settlers in the Wyoming Valley, along the Susquehanna River. Teedyuscung came to be referred to as King of the Delaware. When the English agreed to consider his land claims and compensation, he came to support them against the French. The English provided a home for Teedyuscung in the Wyoming Valley along the north branch of the Susquehanna River. He died there in a tragic fire that destroyed twenty homes. It was rumored that the fires were set by developers who wanted to take the land.

Wangomend (Wangomen) (active 1760s–1790s), shaman, lived among a Munsee band that had moved from New York and New Jersey in the mid-1740s, after the Walking Purchase agreement. He lived in a village called Goshgoshing on the upper reaches of the Allegheny River in present-day northwestern Pennsylvania. As a shaman, he fashioned his own set of beliefs and practices based on traditional Delaware religion. He made notes on a chart, which he consulted when teaching the people. He encouraged the Delaware to return to their traditional ways and renounce those of the settlers, especially drinking whiskey and keeping slaves. Unlike the shaman Papounan, he rejected the teachings of the Moravian missionary David Zeisberger, who was actively trying to convert the Delaware in the 1760s. Wangomend was especially influential as a prophet among his people during the 1790s.

White Eyes (Koquethagechton, Koguethagechton, Kuckquetackton) (ca. 1730–1778), leader, served as principal counselor until he became chief in 1776. He encouraged Delaware neutrality during the American Revolution; but Hopocan, a war chief, sided with the British. To prove his courage, White Eyes led his warriors into battle as allies of the Americans. He told his people that he hoped to die in battle so that he would not witness the destruction of the Delaware people.

In September 1778 he signed the Treaty of Fort Pitt, which was the first agreement between Native American peoples and the young United States republic. The treaty recognized the Delaware Nation and promised congressional representation. In November, while he was serving as a guide for General Lachlan McIntosh's attack against Fort Sandusky, White Eyes was shot by an American soldier. It is unclear why the chief was killed. He possibly had caused conflict because he did not want to take up arms against other Delaware warriors at the fort. However, wishing to keep White Eyes's followers on their side, the soldiers initially reported that he had died of smallpox, which further confused the issue.

Although the Delaware remain spread throughout the United States and Canada, their people's history remains intact. The men and women who have made their names in Delaware history continue to be examples for present and future generations. The Delaware are a persistent tribe that succeeds in the face of obstacles. With continued dedication, the Delaware tribe's historical roots and presence in society will remain for decades to come.

CHRONOLOGY

1524 The Delaware first encounter Europeans when they meet Giovanni da Verrazano as he explores the Atlantic coast.

1609 Henry Hudson sails into what becomes New York State and greater numbers of Europeans begin arriving in Delaware territory.

1630–1767 The Delaware are forced to sign nearly eight hundred agreements in which they surrender most of their homeland, Lenapehoking, to European colonists.

1640–1664 Many Delaware people are killed in a series of conflicts with settlers: the Peach War, Governor Kieft's War, and the Esopus Wars.

1670 The Iroquois claim authority over all the remaining Delaware bands.

1737 The Delaware agree to the Walking Purchase, which leads to the loss of their land in eastern Pennsylvania.

1755 The Delaware ally with the French against the British and the bands become more united.

1758 The Delaware and British sign a peace treaty at Easton, Pennsylvania.

1763 The British drive the French from eastern North America.

1763–1764 Allied Native tribes rise up against the British in Pontiac's Rebellion.

1768 In the Treaty of Fort Stanwix, the Delaware are forced to move north with the Iroquois or west into Ohio.

1776 The Delaware are drawn into the American Revolution.

1778 Chief White Eyes signs a treaty with the thirteen colonies and is killed.

1782 Colonial soldiers massacre peaceful Delaware people at a Moravian settlement called Gnadenhütten in Ohio.

1785 In a treaty with the United States, the Delaware are forced to move farther west.

1790–1791 Many Delaware warriors join Miami chief Little Turtle in a Native alliance against the Americans.

1792 A band of Delaware establishes Moraviantown in Ontario, Canada.

1794 Native confederacy in Little Turtle's War is defeated at Fallen Timbers, Ohio.

1795 In the treaty at Fort Greenville, Ohio, between Native tribes and the United States, the Delaware are forced to surrender all their territory in Ohio.

1818–1840 Delaware bands migrate to Indiana but are subsequently forced to move farther west into Indian Territory (Kansas and Oklahoma).

1859 Delaware people living among the Caddo Tribe in Texas move to Indian Territory and are later federally recognized as the Delaware Tribe of Western Oklahoma (called the Delaware Nation beginning in 2000).

1867 Delaware bands living in Kansas move to eastern Oklahoma and settle among the Cherokee Nation of Oklahoma.

1924 The last complete Big House Ceremony is held in which the spirits of the Delaware homeland are called upon through traditional songs and dances.

1984 Nora Thompson Dean, one of the last great Delaware traditionalists, dies in Oklahoma at age seventy-seven.

1992 The four main Delaware bands—of Muncey, Moraviantown, and eastern and western Oklahoma— agree to revive the Grand Council, a confederacy said to have bound the Delaware together when they were living in Ohio in the eighteenth century.

2013 The Delaware Tribe of Indians of Oklahoma purchases land in Lawrence, Kansas, and establishes a second tribal headquarters there.

2015 The Munsee Delaware continue to fight for more territory.

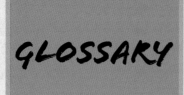

GLOSSARY

Algonquian Most widespread group or "family" of languages spoken in North America. Many Native American tribes speak Algonquian, including the Abenaki, Arapaho, Blackfoot, Cheyenne, Delaware, Fox, and Shawnee.

allotment Government policy, started in 1887, in which reservations were divided and parcels of land were distributed to individuals.

artisan A craftsperson.

breechcloth A cloth or skin worn between the legs; also breechclout.

buckskin Deer hide softened by a curing process known as tanning.

clan A large family group whose members trace their descent from a common ancestor.

confederacy A political, military, and economic union of tribes or nations.

cradleboard A wooden board used to carry a baby.

famine When a country or area does not have enough food to eat.

Gamwing Big House Ceremony.

hoe To dig up earth to prepare for growing crops such as corn.

Indian Removal Act An 1830 law that authorized the relocation of any Native Americans living east of the Mississippi River to Indian Territory in present-day Oklahoma.

Indian Territory Region in the south-central United States, including most of what is now Oklahoma, where the US government relocated many Native American tribes.

Kishëlmukòng Creator, or Great Spirit, of the Delaware, whose name means, "He Who Creates Us by His Thoughts."

Lenape Traditional name of the Delaware.

Lenapehoking Delaware name for their ancestral homeland, meaning "Land of the People."

Mësinghhòlikàn Participants in a dance that honored Mësingw, the spirit that controlled the game hunted by the Delaware.

Mësingw Guardian spirit of deer and other game animals.

mëteìnu Shaman; medicine man or woman.

moccasins Soft leather shoes often decorated with brightly colored beads.

Munsee One of the divisions of the Delaware tribe.

palisade A fence made with large stakes to keep back intruders.

shaman Religious leader responsible for the physical and spiritual well-being of the people in the village.

sweat lodge A dome-shaped hut covered with bark or mats, in which men and women purify themselves.

Unami One of the divisions of the Delaware tribe.

vision quest Religious undertaking by an adolescent boy, who leaves the village and fasts in isolation in hopes of finding his guardian spirit in a dream.

Xingwikaon Structure in which the Delaware held ceremonies to maintain their traditions. Also known as the Big House.

BIBLIOGRAPHY

Boyd, Paul D. *Atlantic Highlands: From Lenape Camps to Bayside Town.* Making of America. Charleston, SC: Arcadia Publishing, 2004.

Carman, Alan E. *Footprints in Time: A History and Ethnology of the Lenape-Delaware Indian Culture.* Bloomington, IN: Trafford, 2013.

Churchill, Ward. *Kill the Indian, Save the Man: The Genocidal Impact of American Indian Residential Schools.* San Francisco, CA: City Lights Publishers, 2004.

Clever, George. *Lenape Animal Tales.* Indianapolis, IN: Dog Ear Publishing, 2014.

Dalton, Anne. *The Lenape of Pennsylvania, New Jersey, New York, Delaware, Wisconsin, Oklahoma, and Ontario.* The Library of Native Americans. New York: PowerKids Press, 2005.

Dunbar-Oritz, Roxanne. *An Indigenous Peoples' History of the United States.* ReVisioning American History. Boston, MA: Beacon Press, 2014.

Fur, Gunlög. *A Nation of Women: Gender and Colonial Encounters Among the Delaware Indians*. Early American Studies. Philadelphia, PA: University of Pennsylvania Press, 2012.

Grumet, Robert S. *The Munsee Indians: A History*. Civilization of the American Indian Series. Norman, OK: University of Oklahoma Press, 2009.

Harp, David W., and Tom Horton. *The Nanticoke: Portrait of a Chesapeake River*. Baltimore, MD: Johns Hopkins University Press, 2008.

Jacobson, Ryan. *William Penn: Founder of Pennsylvania*. Graphic Biographies. North Mankato, MN: Capstone Press, 2006.

Marsh, Dawn G. *A Lenape Among the Quakers: The Life of Hannah Freeman*. Lincoln, NE: University of Nebraska Press, 2014.

Murdoch, David S. *North American Indian*. DK Eyewitness Books. New York: DK Children, 2005.

Oberly, James W. *A Nation of Statesmen: The Political Culture of the Stockbridge-Munsee Mohicans, 1815–1972*. Civilization of the American Indian Series. Norman, OK: University of Oklahoma Press, 2005.

Obermeyer, Brice. *Delaware Tribe in a Cherokee Nation*. Lincoln, NE: University of Nebraska Press, 2009.

Schutt, Amy C. *Peoples of the River Valleys: The Odyssey of the Delaware Indians*. Early American Studies. Philadelphia, PA: University of Pennsylvania Press, 2007.

Soderlund, Jean R. *Lenape Country: Delaware Valley Society Before William Penn*. Early American Studies. Philadelphia, PA: University of Pennsylvania Press, 2015.

Weslager, C.A. *Delaware's Forgotten Folk: The Story of the Moors and Nanticokes*. Philadelphia, PA: University of Pennsylvania Press, 2006.

FURTHER INFORMATION

Want to know more about the Delaware Nation? Check out these websites, videos, and organizations.

Websites

Lenape Lifeways

www.lenapelifeways.org

This website gives information and videos about Lenape life in the early days of the tribe.

Removal of the Delaware Tribe from Native Lands

www.delawaretribe.org/services-and-programs/historic-preservation/removal-history-of-the-delaware-tribe

This website gives the history of the removal of the Delaware Tribe from their original territory.

Turtle Children: Learn to Speak Lenape

www.delawarenation.com/History/TurtleChildren/tabid/99/Default.aspx

This website features key phrases and pronunciation guides to help you learn to speak Lenape.

Videos

Dance with Me: The Nanticoke Lenni-Lenape Indians of New Jersey

www.youtube.com/watch?v=PQ8M8Y4SiZM

This video features interviews with some of the Nanticoke tribe members and explores how Native culture remains visible today.

Delaware Nation Documentary

www.youtube.com/watch?v=iWFeMGmJne4

This video explores the Delaware Nation's past and present.

The Lenape Culture: Vision Quest

www.youtube.com/watch?v=U5P1EgQZJHY

This video explains the importance of vision quests to the Lenape people.

Return to Kansas

www.youtube.com/watch?v=bY0nznd3pgA

This is the story of the Delaware Tribe today, as told by tribal members.

Organizations

Delaware Nation
PO Box 825
Anadarko, OK 73005
(405) 247-2448
www.delawarenation.com

Delaware Nation at Moraviantown
14760 School House Line
RR #3
Thamesville, ON N0P 2K0
Canada
(519) 692-3936
www.delawarenation.on.ca

The Delaware Tribe of Indians
Delaware Tribal Headquarters
5100 Tuxedo Blvd
Bartlesville, OK 74006
(918) 337-6590
www.delawaretribe.org

The Lenape Nation
PO Box 43
Saylosrburg, PA 18353
www.lenapenation.org

Munsee-Delaware Nation
Thames River
RR #1
Muncey, ON N0L 1Y0
Canada
(519) 289-5396
www.munseedelawarenation.org

Nanticoke Lenni-Lenape Indians of New Jersey
18 East Commerce Street
Bridgeton, NJ 08302
(856) 455-6910
www.nanticoke-lenape.info

Ramapough Lunaape Nation
189 Stag Hill Rd.
Mahwah, NJ 07430
(201) 529-1171
www.ramapoughlenapenation.org

Thunder Mountain Lenape Nation
236 Skyline Dr.
Saltsburg, PA 15681
(724) 639-3488
www.thundermtnlenape.org

INDEX

Page numbers in **boldface** are illustrations. Entries in **boldface** are glossary terms.

housing, 15, 23–26, **24–25, 26**

   See also longhouse;
wigwam

Hudson, Henry, 14

Hudson River, 16–17, 19, 41, 70, 104

hunting, 13, 15, 21-22, 25, 27, 29, 32–33, 37, 39–41, 50, 55, 57

Indiana, 74–75, 85–86

Indian Removal Act, 75

Indian Territory, 74–75, 86, 98, 101

Iroquois, 27, 36, **36–37**, 38, 61, 73, 103, 107

Jacobs, 100

Jamestown, 11–12

jewelry, 46, 57

Journeycake, Charles, 100–101, **101**

Kansas, 56, 61, 74–75, 86, 88, 101

Kishëlmukòng, 54–55

language, 10, 16–17, **18**, 19, 21, 61, 76, 78–80, 86, 92, 101

Lappawinsoe, 73, 102–103, **102**, 107

Lenape, 11–13, 16, 56, 61, 64, 86, **87**, 89,

Lenapehoking, 16

Logan, James, 71, 102

longhouse, 23–25, **68**

Mahican, **18**, 22, 76, 107

marriage, 22–23, 27, 32, 34–35

Marshall, Edward, 73, 102

medicine, 35, 62–63

Mësinghhòlikàn, 55

mëteìnu, 62

Mexican War, 96

missionaries, 55–57, **56**, 61, 78, 97, **97**, 105–108

moccasins, 44, 46, 48

Mohawk, **18**, 22, 36

Moravians, 55–56, 74, 99–100, 105, 107–108

Moraviantown, 75, 91–92

Muncey, 61, 91

Munsee, 16–17, 27, 63, 75–76, 78, 91, 104, 108

Munsee Delaware Nation, 61, 91

Muskingum River, 73, 99, 105

ABOUT THE AUTHOR

Raymond Bial has published more than eighty books—most of them photography books—during his career. His photo-essays for children include *Corn Belt Harvest, Amish Home, Frontier Home, Shaker Home, The Underground Railroad, Portrait of a Farm Family, With Needle and Thread: A Book About Quilts, Mist Over the Mountains: Appalachia and Its People, Cajun Home,* and *Where Lincoln Walked.*

As with his other work, Bial's deep feeling for his subjects is evident in both the text and illustrations. He travels to tribal cultural centers, photographing homes, artifacts, and surroundings and learning firsthand about the national lifeways of these peoples.

The emeritus director of a small college library in the Midwest, he lives with his wife and three children in Urbana, Illinois.